PAINLESS ARRANGING
FOR OLD TIME
COUNTRY GUITAR

by

Joe Weidlich

ISBN 978-1-57424-257-7
SAN 683-8022

Cover Photos (clockwise from the left): Rouse Bros.; Irvin & Gordon, The Allen Brothers, Unkown, Unkown, Unkown Guitarist, The Rail Splitters

Cover Design by James Creative Group

❦ Preface ❦

The purpose of *Painless Arranging for Old Time Country Guitar* is simple: it will help the reader to visually recognize commonly used note patterns in fiddle tunes and string band music by giving those patterns an identification label, thus making it easier to memorize them as related musical units. These principal note sequences include Turns, Chord Tone Connectors, Digital Patterns, Scale Fragments, and Chord Outlines. Once it is understood how those patterns and note sequences are used, one can then begin to use them <u>painlessly</u> to create interesting variations.

The author, Joseph Weidlich, briefly analyses four traditional fiddle tunes showing how some of these note sequences are used in them. He then looks at each of those note sequences in more detail, showing how notes or patterns can be substituted, later demonstrating how one can <u>painlessly</u> construct variations using the famous string band song, *The Wreck of the Old 97*, as the platform. In all, he improvises three choruses explaining along the way the thinking behind his note choices.

Of related interest by Joseph Weidlich are *Old-Time Country Guitar Backup Basics* (based on commercial recordings of the 1920s and early 1930s), *Guitar Backup Styles of Southern String Bands from the Golden Age of Phonograph Recordings*, which features the guitar backup styles of Ernest Stoneman's Dixie Mountaineers, the Carter Family, Charlie Poole and the North Carolina Ramblers, Gid Tanner and the Skillet Lickers, and Jimmie Rodgers (often acknowledged as "the father of country music"), *Memphis Blues & Ragtime Guitar Backup* (based on the recordings of The Memphis String Band, Gus Cannon's Jug Stompers and The Beale Street Sheiks), and *The Country Guitar Style of Charlie Monroe* (based on the 1936-1938 Bluebird Recordings by The Monroe Brothers). He has also written *String Band Banjo Styles*, which presents an overview of the basic banjo styles used in the 1920s and early 1930s string band genre with an emphasis on the transition from thumb-lead to early 3-finger roll patterns and their usage. These books are all available from Centerstream Publishing, Anaheim, California.

Georgia Peach Pickers

❧ Table of Contents ❧

Biography

Joseph Weidlich [b. 1945] began his formal musical studies on the classic guitar. He moved to Washington, D.C. in 1972, from his native St. Louis, to teach classic guitar at The Guitar Shop (estb. 1922 by Sophocles Papas). During the 1970s he performed in several classic guitar master classes conducted by notable students of Andres Segovia. He has also played renaissance guitar, renaissance lute, and baroque guitar in the early music genre.

In 1978, he completed research on and writing of an article on *Battuto Performance Practice in Early Italian Guitar Music (1606-1637)*, for the Journal of the Lute Society of America, 1978 (Volume XI). That article outlined the various strumming practices, with numerous examples, found in early guitar methods published in Italy and Spain in the early 17th century. In the late 1970s he also published a series of renaissance lute transcriptions for classic guitar, published by DeCamera Publishing Company, Washington, D.C., which were distributed by G. Schirmer, New York/London.

The banjo has also been no stranger in Joe's musical life. He began learning various folk banjo styles in the late 1950s-early 1960s during the folk music boom, later learning to play plectrum jazz and classic banjo styles as well. His extensive research in the history of minstrel banjo demonstrates how that style formed the foundation of clawhammer banjo. Alan Jabbour, noted old-time fiddler, musicologist and former long-time director of the Library of Congress' American Folklife Center, has said of Joe's book, *The Early Minstrel Banjo: Its Technique and Repertoire*, that "our understanding of the minstrel banjo in the 19th century is greatly enhanced by the long labors you have devoted to the subject and the fine understanding you have brought to it." On a related issue, The American Banjo Fraternity published an article Joe authored on James Buckley's *New Banjo Book* [1860] in their newsletter, the *Five-Stringer*, #185, Double Issue, Fall-Winter 2000-01. Joe also collaborated with banjo builder Mike Ramsey (Chanterelle Workshop) in designing two prototype minstrel banjos based on the dimensions described in Phil Rice's *Correct Method* [1858], as well as similar instruments made by William Boucher in Baltimore in the 1840s.

Also published by Centerstream Publishing are Joe's editions of George Knauff's *Virginia Reels* [1839] arranged for guitar, believed to be the only substantial extant compilation of nineteenth-century Southern fiddle tunes published in the South prior to the Civil War (which includes songs later featured in the early minstrel shows), *Minstrel Banjo—Brigg's Banjo Instructor* [1855], *More Minstrel Banjo*--Frank Converse's *Banjo Instructor, Without A Master* [1865], *Old-Time Country Guitar Backup Basics* (based on commercial recordings of the 1920s and early 1930s), *Guitar Backup Styles of Southern String Bands from the Golden Age of Phonograph Recordings*, which features the guitar backup styles of Ernest Stoneman's Dixie Mountaineers, the Carter Family, Charlie Poole and the North Carolina Ramblers, Gid Tanner and the Skillet Lickers, and Jimmie Rodgers (often acknowledged as "the father of country music"), *Memphis Blues & Ragtime Guitar Backup* (based on the recordings of The Memphis String Band, Gus Cannon's Jug Stompers and The Beale Street Sheiks), *Painless Arranging for Old-Time Country Guitar*, and *The Country Guitar Style of Charlie Monroe* (based on the 1936-1938 Bluebird Recordings by The Monroe Brothers). He has also written *String Band Banjo Styles*, which presents an overview of the basic banjo styles used in the 1920s and early 1930s string band genre with an emphasis on the transition from thumb-lead to early 3-finger roll patterns and their usage.

In the jazz genre, Joseph Weidlich has written *Swing Era Rhythm Guitar: Beyond the Basics; The Guitar Chord Shapes of Charlie Christian; Trading Licks: Charlie Christian and T-Bone Walker*, and *Bebop Guitar: Basic Theory and Practice for Jazz Guitar in the Style of Charlie Parker*.

Part I: Introduction

Welcome to *Painless Arranging for Old Time Country Guitar!* The purpose of this book is simple: it will help you to recognize commonly used note patterns in string band music by giving those patterns a name, i.e., an identification label, making it easer for you to memorize the individual notes as a related musical pattern; then, once you understand how those note sequences are used, you can begin to use them painlessly to create variations in fiddle tunes or songs. I will initially provide examples of how these note sequences are used in fiddle tunes, as they are frequently constructed of chord outlines and basic scale fragments.

Here are the principal note sequences that I will be discussing in this book:

> Turns (3-beat figures)
> Chord Tone Connectors (3-beat figures)
> Digital Patterns (2-beat figures)
> Scale Fragments (e.g., spins, tetra [4-note] chords)
> Chord Outlines

I will provide additional variations on these basic note sequences as we go along, so let's get started!

Turns.

A turn is a 3-beat, 5-note figure in which the first, third and last notes of the sequence are identical, e.g., the Root of a scale. In such cases the normal note sequence consists of Root – lower neighbor tone – Root – upper diatonic neighbor tone – Root. The initial lower neighbor tone is usually a half step below the Root, i.e., the leading tone of the major scale. Here is an example in C Major:

You will occasionally find a turn using the neighbor tones in reverse order:

When using the latter turn figure the following note sequence is a nice variation to consider using:

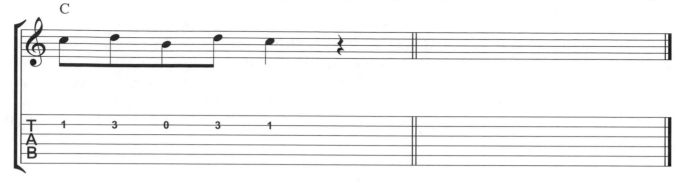

Chord Tone Connectors.

This note sequence is a 3-beat, 5-note figure which <u>connects</u> <u>notes</u> that are the interval of a third apart, ascending <u>or</u> descending. It is very similar in appearance to a turn except for the concluding note in the sequence. For instance, if the melodic line moves from C up to E, then the fourth note moves upwards to E, rather than back to the Root, C:

When the note sequence descends an interval of a third the opposite movement occurs:

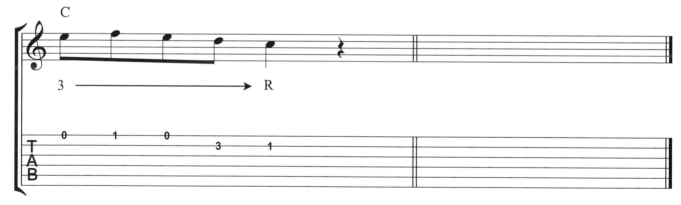

That was painless, wasn't it?   Let's move on to the family of digital patterns.

Digital Patterns.

Digital patterns are usually 2-beat, 4-note figures in which the first and last notes of the pattern are the same, thus very useful for tunes performed in Common time. There are a wide variety of digital patterns in use; here are some of the more commonly used ones:

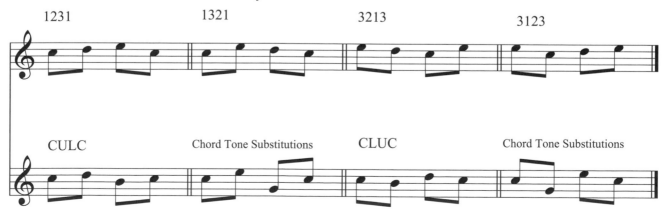

I will discuss these patterns in more detail as we work our way through this material.

Scale Fragments.

Scale fragments are parts, or fragments, of scale lines. Let's begin by looking at a note sequence called a spin, i.e., the notes "spin" away from and back to the initial note, usually not larger that the interval of a Perfect Fifth (ascending) or Perfect Fourth (descending). Spins are often used to "fill up" dead space. Here are the basic examples, ascending and descending:

Chord Outlines.

These are basically arpeggio figures so I will point them out in the examples as we go along. As you are aware of, a lot of fiddle tunes are based on chord outlines, such as *Soldier's Joy*.

Music Theory and Practice. Now that I have outlined some of the basic note sequences let me present a few fiddle tunes showing their use in context:

Peacemakers Hornpipe

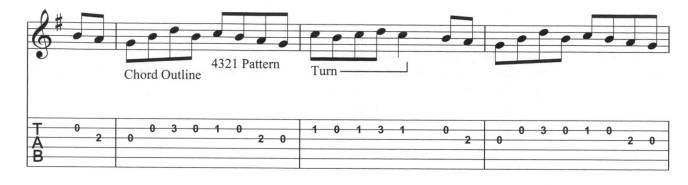

Chord Outline 4321 Pattern Turn

C/T Connector + Tag

1231 Pattern

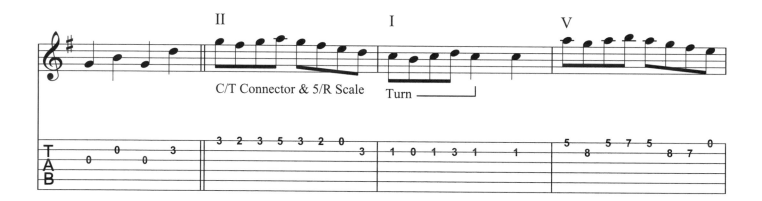

II I V

C/T Connector & 5/R Scale Turn

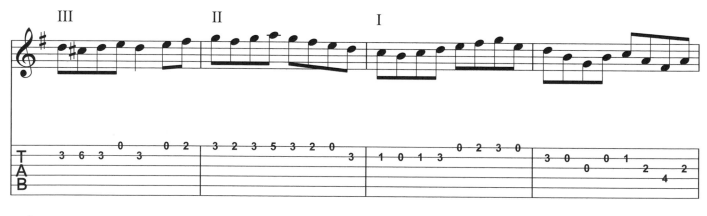

III II I

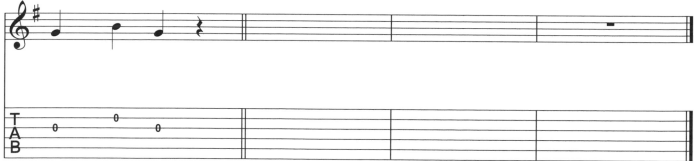

The Dorsetshire Hornpipe

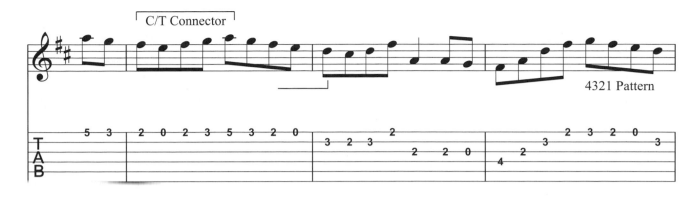

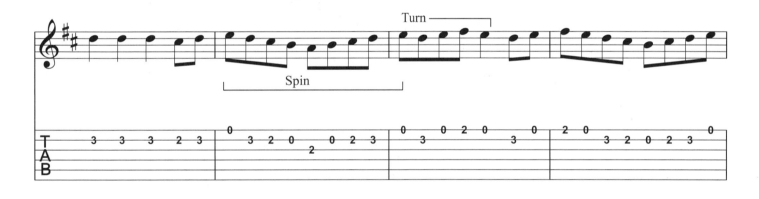

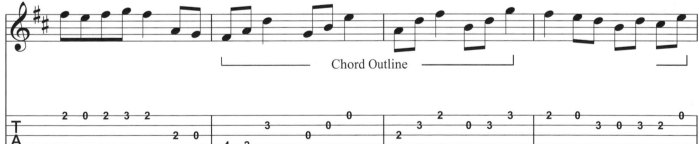

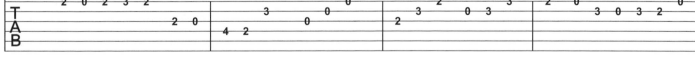

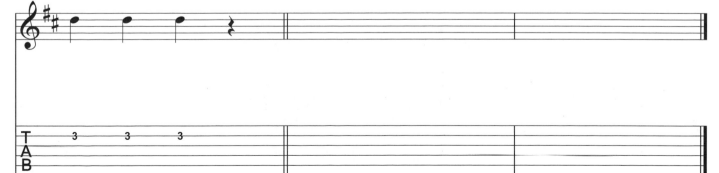

Corn Rigs

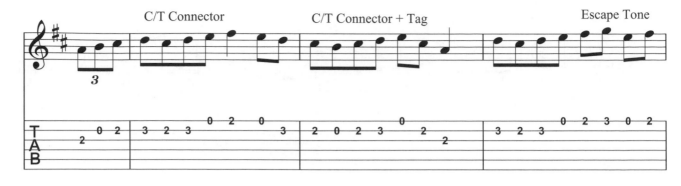

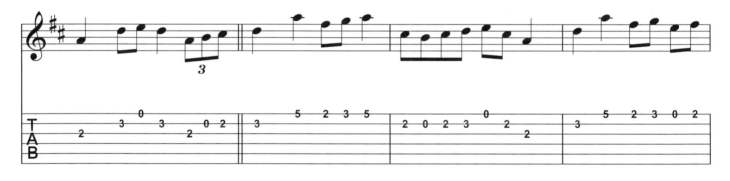

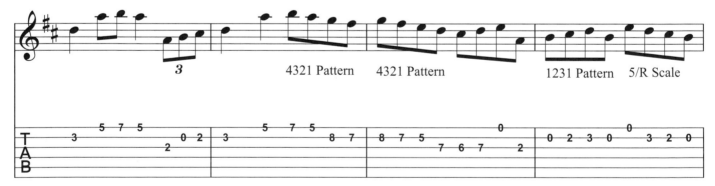

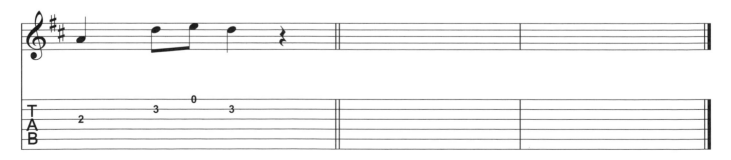

Bonny Kate

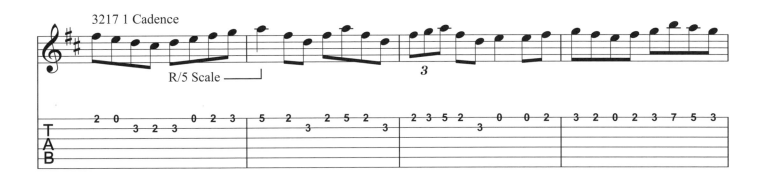

Now that I have briefly outlined some of the commonly used note sequences, let's look at them more closely.

Turns.

As we have seen, the turn note sequence is usually a 5-note figure, the first and last notes being the same; this is also characteristic among many digital patterns as well.

Let's look at some usages of the turn with the principal note being the Root of the chord. Here is a typical example when the turn is positioned on the downbeat at a cadence:

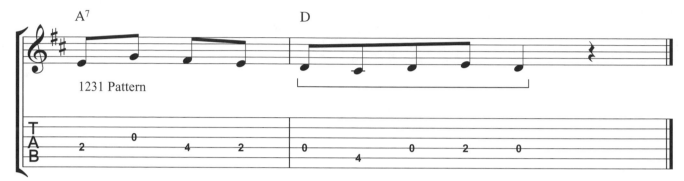

Here, a turn is positioned on the downbeat which ends with a 1321 digital pattern tag which is used to fill in space after the arrival of C on beat 3:

The use of the 1321 digital pattern as a concluding tag is also quite common.

Turns can easily be used to substitute for chord outlines. Here is such an example (note that the first and fifth notes in the measure are the same, C):

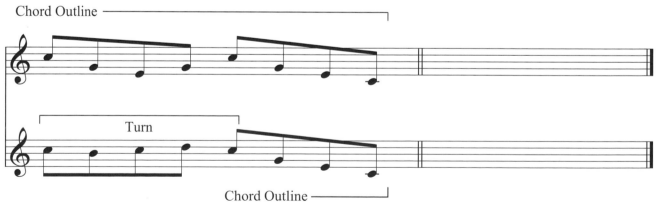

Chord tone notes can be used to painlessly substitute for one of the notes in the turn figure. In the following example the principal note is the third of the C chord, E; the second note of the figure is changed from E's upper neighbor tone, F, to the next higher chord tone, G (the Fifth of the C chord):

Now, let's look at a turn figure where the Fifth of the D chord is positioned on the downbeat, this time used at a half cadence phrase ending:

Turns can also be used to connect the same chord. In the following example the G chord is used to connect two C chords, thus acting as a passing chord. The turn, based on the Fifth of the G chord, D, segues into a scale fragment that I usually label as *5/R Scale* because the note sequence begins on the fifth of the Tonic chord and ends on the Root:

The initial lower neighbor note of the turn, i.e., the second note, <u>is</u> <u>not</u> <u>always</u> a half-step below the principal note (depending on which chord tone begins the turn figure). Experiment using the diatonic lower note or the chromatic half-step and see how that "sound" contributes to or detracts from the phrase that it is used in.

Now, here is an example where two turn figures, both based on the Root of their respective chords, G and C, are connected by the 5/R Scale fragment that I just discussed:

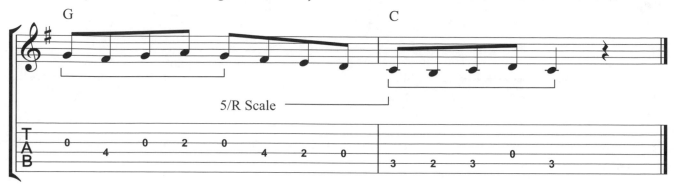

Regarding this transition make note of the fact that the first note of this descending scale fragment is the Root of the Dominant chord (G in this example); when it appears on beat 3 it could also be analyzed as the Fifth of the C Major scale, as I mentioned the 5/R Scale fragment connector. This function of such a note is labeled as "common tone" because the same note can be analyzed differently in the same context based on the harmonic structure.

Next is an example where a 5-note descending scale spin leads to a turn figure, both note sequences based on the Fifth of the A chord, E:

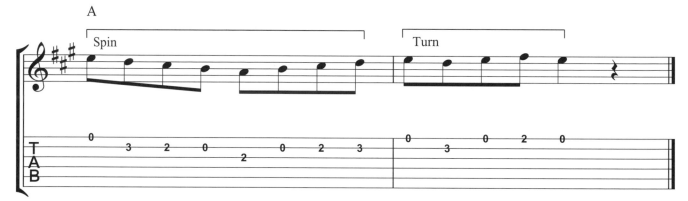

Next is an intriguing turn figure in which the initial note is based not on the Root of the scale, this time C, but on the second note of the C Major scale, D:

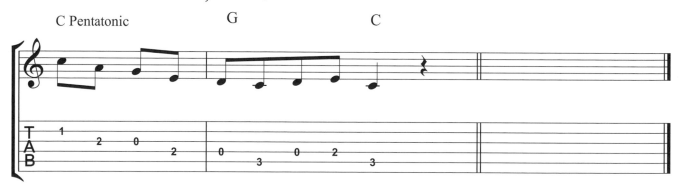

This type of turn figure is usually found only at final cadences.

Here is an example of how Doc Watson transforms a stock pentatonic note lick into a turn figure by simply changing the second note of the sequence, a very useful substitution:

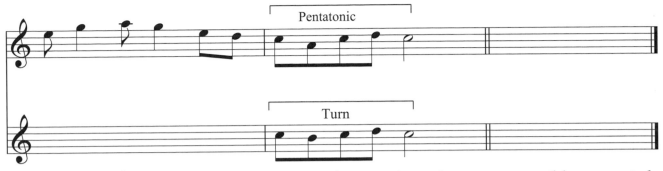

As you can see, the simple turn note figure can be used in a variety of ways to smoothly connect chords or to end phrases. Let's move on now to the cousin of the turn, what I call a Chord Tone Connector note sequence (often abbreviated as *C/T Connector* in this book).

Chord Tone Connectors.

As noted earlier, the principal difference between the chord tone connector and the turn figure is that the final note differs from the initial note. The initial note of a chord tone connector figure can be based on any chord tone, be that note the Root, Third, etc.; also, as in the turn figure, chord tones are often substituted for the second note in the sequence. An easy way to understand this figure is that it is simply based on neighbor and passing tones in an ascending diatonic scale passage:

The second note of the connector phrase dictates the direction of the note sequence: if that note is the lower neighbor tone, diatonic or chromatic, then the figure ascends; if the second note is above the principal note then the figure will descend towards the lower chord tone.

Chord tones can be substituted for the second note in this sequence. Here is an example used in an ascending chord tone connector figure:

Next is a similar comparison, this time in a descending chord tone connector note sequence:

There are a couple of additional painless substitutions which you can use. Instead of using the standard ascending C/T connector figure, this example makes use of the lower tetra chord scale fragment, e.g., from the Root ascending to the Fourth, which results in a 4-3 suspension figure:

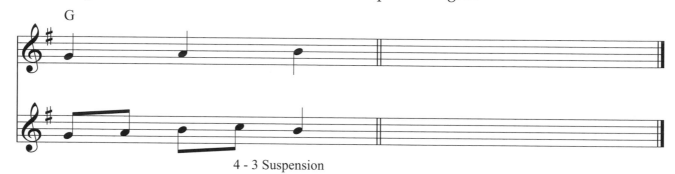

4 - 3 Suspension

A related substitution is based on the 1231 digital pattern which changes the third and fourth notes of the figure (the "1" in the pattern simply means the initial note):

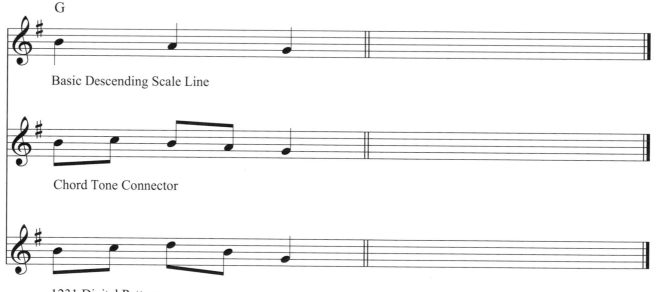

Basic Descending Scale Line

Chord Tone Connector

1231 Digital Pattern

When the first note of a descending Chord Tone Connector is the Third, then a digital pattern I call 3217 1 can be painlessly substituted. Here is a comparison:

Chord Tone Connector

3217 1 Cadence

When a scale descends by the interval of a third a useful variation, based on what is called an escape tone note sequence, works quite nicely. I will discuss the theory of the escape tone figure later on, but here is an example of its use as a substitute for a descending chord tone connector figure:

Escape Tone Note Sequence

Here is how a stock pentatonic note sequence can be substituted for a descending Chord Tone connector, yet another painless variation:

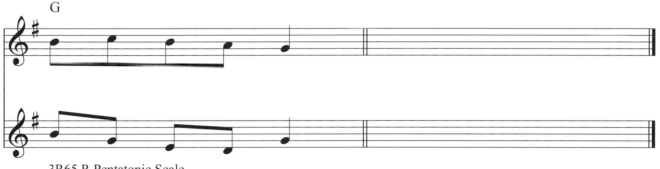

3R65 R Pentatonic Scale

I suggest that you make note of these substitutions as you encounter them for future reference.

Rhythmic variation can be used <u>to</u> <u>disguise</u> a chord tone connector figure. Here is an example in a descending figure beginning on the Third of the C chord, E:

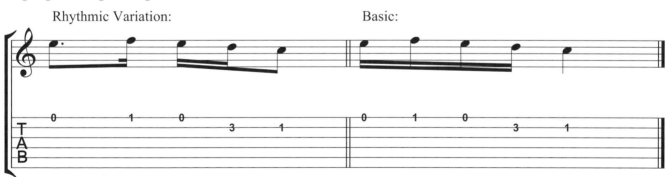

What happens if you only have two beats to fit in a stock C/T connector sequence? That is easily accomplished by simply eliminating the fourth note of the sequence. Here is a comparison:

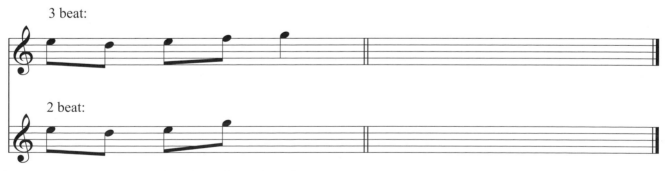

As you have seen, many variations on the Chord Tone connector note sequence can be used. You have heard them or seen them written out many times, but perhaps you just didn't know how to analyze and/or use them: the age-old axiom of theory vs. practice. Thus, instead of learning five seemingly unrelated notes you now know how to incorporate them as a single note sequence. Now, let's look at some additional examples in context.

3-beat Chord Tone Connector Examples.

Here is an example where a Chord Tone connector based on C <u>leads to</u> the V chord, G:

While a 1321 digital pattern tag was not used at the end of the initial measure it could have been because the notes on beats 3 and 4 of that measure are the same, E (i.e., the "1" in this pattern).

In the next example a 3213 digital pattern is used as a tag instead of the more commonly used 3123 pattern:

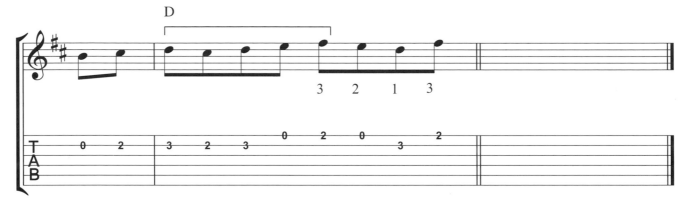

Next, an ascending chord tone connector leads to an escape tone figure which leads back to the Root of the D chord (although a descending chord tone connector could just as easily have been used):

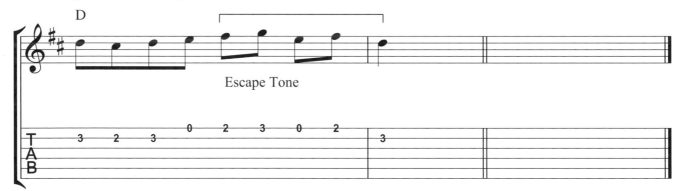

Since the total number of beats in the previous example equals 5, i.e., downbeat to the following downbeat, a descending scale spin could also have been used, as show below:

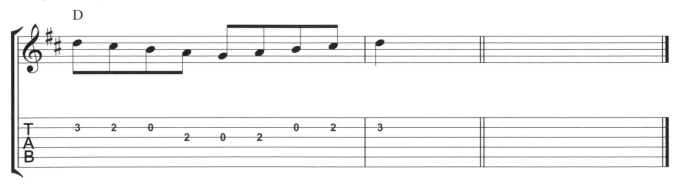

Let's look at a cadential figure where a couple of additional figures could be used. Because the Third of the C chord, E, is positioned on the downbeat, a 3217 1 digital pattern or a 3R65 R descending pentatonic note sequence could have be used.

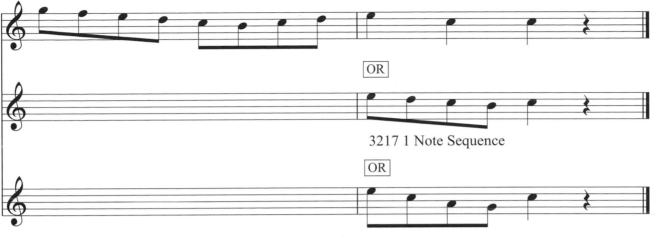

3217 1 Note Sequence

3R65 R Pentatonic Note Sequence

In the next example the 3217 1 note sequence is used <u>to</u> <u>lead</u> <u>to</u> an ascending Chord Tone connector figure (note that a descending Chord Tone connector could also replace the 3217 1 pattern used here, thus two consecutive connector figures in contrary motion):

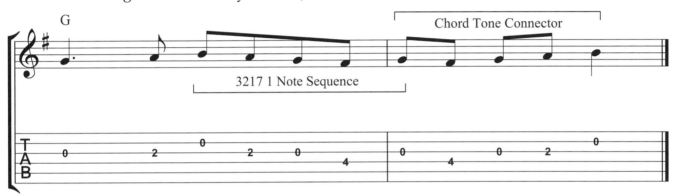

The 2-beat Chord Tone Connector Substitute.

In the following example the use of consecutive Chord tone connectors in one measure is not possible; therefore, the abbreviated 2-beat chord tone connector form is used to follow the initial C to E Chord Tone connector sequence (as noted earlier, the fourth note of the stock connector figure is not played in its abbreviated version):

Chord tones can also be substituted in 2-beat Chord Tone connector note sequences, often transforming them into a chord outline figures as a result:

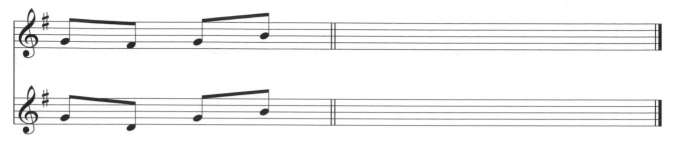

Converted to chord outline

Now, let's look at a few examples of how Doc Watson uses this figure in his playing:

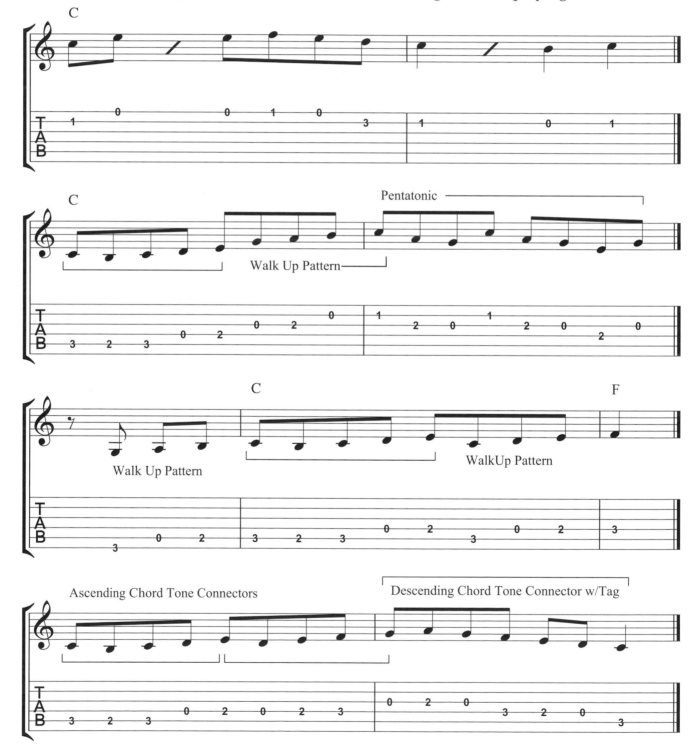

In this example Watson begins by using a descending Chord Tone connector based on the Root of the F chord descending to its submediant sixth scale degree, D; he then reverses the sequence (which then strongly resembles <u>an inverted</u> 3217 1 figure):

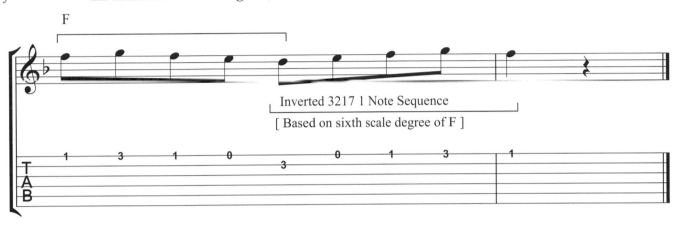

Scales.

As melodies are often based on scales and/or chord outlines, we need to look at the scales and scale fragments frequently found in fiddle tunes. The most basic scale found in folk cultures around the world is the pentatonic scale, so our journey begins there.

The Pentatonic Scale.

The easiest way to understand this scale is to think of it as a Major diatonic scale <u>without</u> the half-steps between scale degrees 3-4 and 7-8. That leaves us with the Root and the scale tones of the second, third, fifth and sixth. Here is the basic G pentatonic scale, ascending and descending:

The fifth note of the pentatonic scale is often used to directly target the arrival of the Root, often positioned on the downbeat of the following measure. The use of the sixth scale tone is commonly used to smoothly bridge this leap of a fourth while creating a stock walk-up pattern in the process:

When the pentatonic scale descends from the octave note, the second note, called the supertonic, is often omitted:

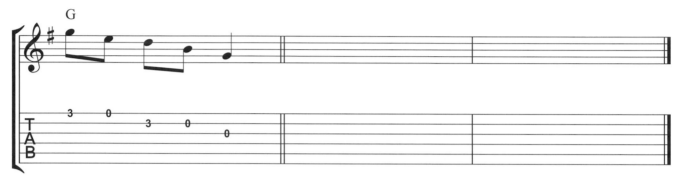

Another useful pattern is the 1235 digital pattern, i.e., the first four notes of the ascending pentatonic scale; this pattern is frequently used to outline a chord. Here it outlines a G Major chord:

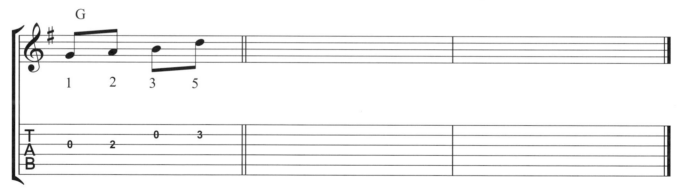

This pattern can also be positioned on the fifth scale degree of the tonic chord to target the octave from a whole step above. Here is an example:

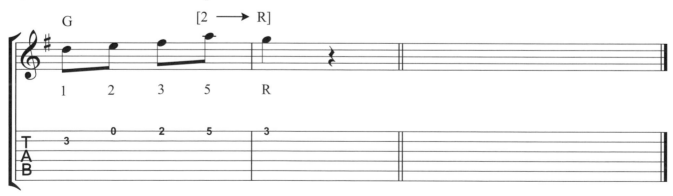

Note that the fifth of the tonic chord acts as a Common Tone with the Root of the dominant chord in diatonic harmony, thus a common tone. The resulting sound is identical but the harmonic analysis necessarily differs.

The 3217 1 cadential pattern (which will be discussed in more detail under the section on Digital Patterns) is easily converted into a pentatonic scale by substituting the sixth scale degree for the seventh (7) scale degree:

At cadences where the third of the tonic chord is positioned on the downbeat a 3R65 R pentatonic 2-beat fragment can also be painlessly substituted:

Now, let's look at a couple of examples where a descending pentatonic scale fragment, that I call R653, is used. In the first example an escape tone figure leads to this fragment which then resolves into what I call a Turn Cadence (2R23 R):

In this example the R653 pentatonic scale fragment leads to a turn based on the Fifth of the D chord, using a diatonic lower neighbor tone instead of the chromatic half step, G#:

Let me next present a 2-measure example that is made up entirely of notes from the pentatonic scale:

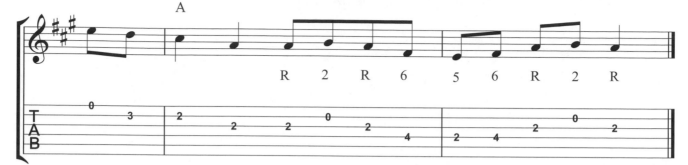

Finally, the 56 R cadential note sequence mentioned earlier can be modified by including use of the leading tone to "lead back" to the Root. This is a very common feature in Doc Watsons's performance style:

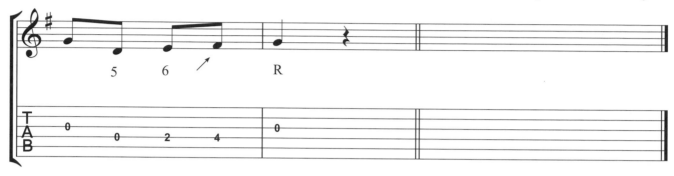

Let's move on now to the Major diatonic scale.

The Major Diatonic Scale.

There are several basic ways that complete diatonic scales can be incorporated into fiddle tunes and songs. The most obvious way is to play the 8-note scale in one measure. In the following example a descending D major scale, with the Root positioned on the downbeat, leads to the G tonic target note:

What if the initial note is the fifth of the V chord? In that case the scale <u>leads</u> <u>directly</u> to the Root of the C chord:

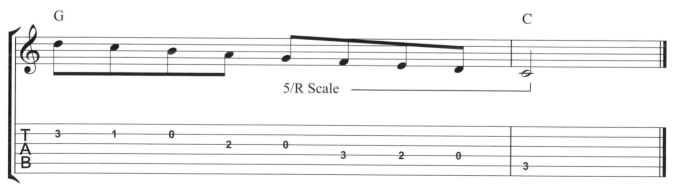

If the rhythm is altered so that the initial note of the ascending scale is a quarter note instead of an eighth note, then the arrival of the octave note will be positioned on the following downbeat:

A variation on this idea is created by playing the Root immediately followed by the octave note, then descending back to the Root:

A similar idea on the previous example is created by substituting the fifth note of the scale on the downbeat instead of the Root:

In this example the supertonic note is positioned on the downbeat leading to the octave note, and then the scale descends to the Root:

The fifth note in a descending scale can be repeated, <u>or</u> tied:

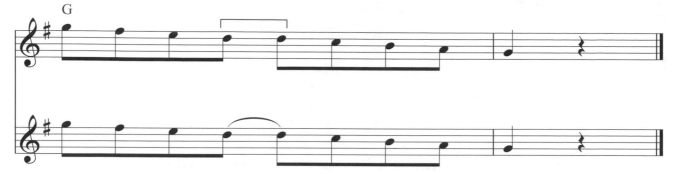

Chromaticism can be used by introducing the use of either the flatted sixth or flatted fifth scale degree:

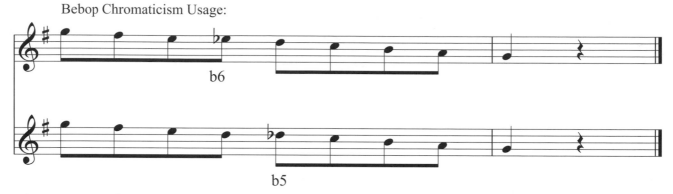

The use of such chromatically altered notes on those scale degrees, while often associated with bebop, were also regularly used by guitarists in the Memphis jug bands of the late 1920s and early 1930s.

R/5 Scale Fragment.
Scale fragments are frequently used in fiddle tunes. One of the most common is the note sequence which begins on the Root (usually positioned on the downbeat of a measure) which <u>then</u> <u>ascends</u> to the fifth of the scale (I often abbreviate this usage as *R/5 Scale* in this book).

In the following example, after this scale fragment arrives at the fifth scale degree it then ascends to the octave note via an ascending Chord Tone connector figure:

Here is an example along the same lines except that the target note is also the Root, the point of departure:

Here is an example where the R/5 Scale fragment is followed by a chord outline tag:

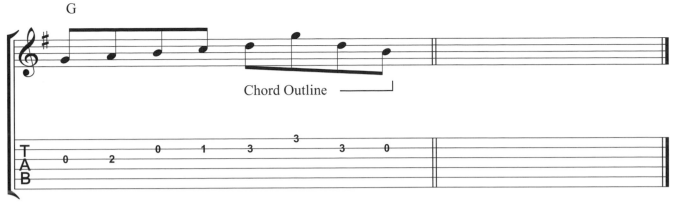

In the following V-I chord change a 1321 pattern is used as a tag to arrive at the target note, G, from the supertonic scale degree; however, an altered Turn Cadence sequence can also have been used:

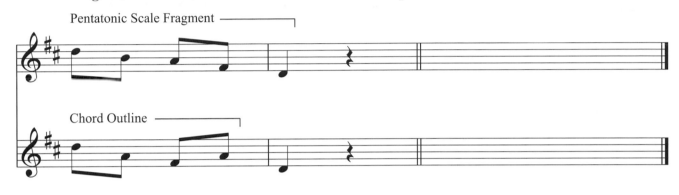

5/R Scale Fragment.

The scale fragment from the fifth descending to the Root (*5/R Scale*) is also commonly employed, often positioned on beat three in a measure, leading to a phrase-ending cadence on the following downbeat:

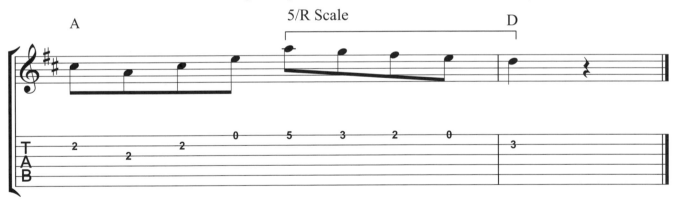

In the following example a turn figure over the D chord leads to this 5/R Scale fragment:

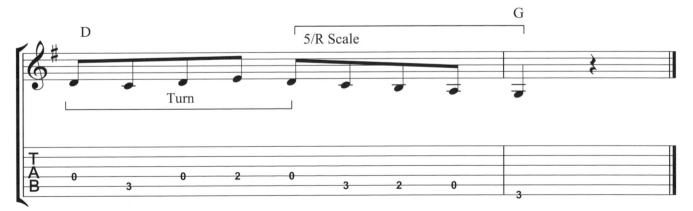

Similarly, a scale spin could have been used to lead to that 5/R Scale fragment:

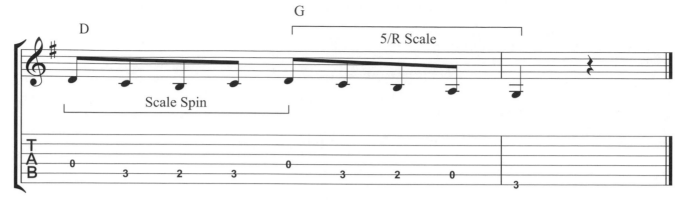

In this example, a pair of descending 5/R Scale fragments are used:

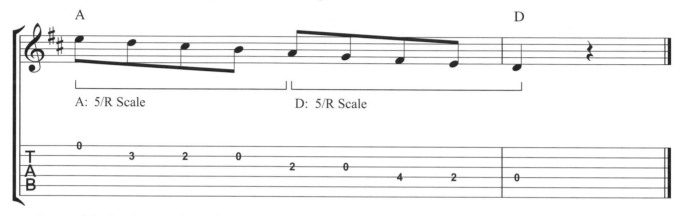

This example could also be analyzed as a descending D major scale beginning on its supertonic, as shown earlier, <u>except</u> that the harmony for the descending scale is based on the A Major scale, <u>not</u> the D Major scale.

Next is an interesting example which demonstrates the use of a 5/R scale immediately followed by a R/5 Scale (which could also be analyzed as a scale spin except for the fact that there would be a change in the harmony midway through the spin fragment); a 1231 digital pattern tag concludes the phrase:

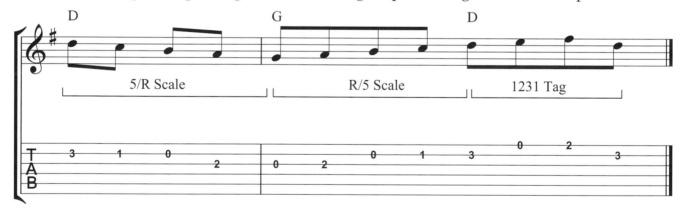

The next 2-measure example in the key of A initially uses a rhythmically-altered 2-note scale spin followed by a 5/R Scale that, in turn, leads to an ascending full octave major diatonic scale:

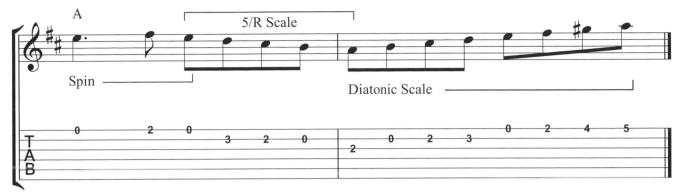

In the following 2-measure IV-I chord change the initial harmony is based on the third of the A chord (this could also be labeled as a "3/3 Scale," i.e., the third scale degree begins and ends the note sequence) followed by a 5/R Scale fragment in the key of E that concludes, once again, with that ever popular 1231 digital pattern tag figure:

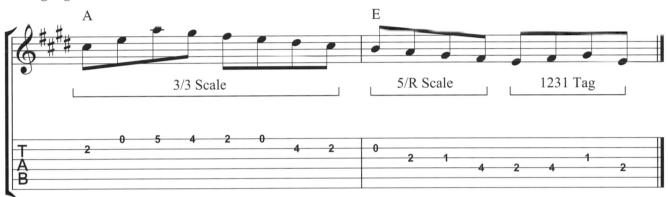

Now, let's look at two ways that Doc Watson used the 5/R Scale fragment. The first example is based on a stationary C chord:

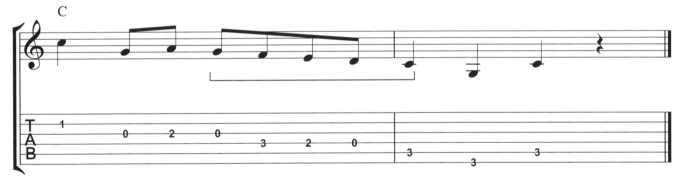

The next example is a little more intricate as it begins with a 3213 digital pattern over C Major, followed by a 5/R Scale over the G7 chord that segues to a 1235 digital pattern targeting the Root of the C tonic chord:

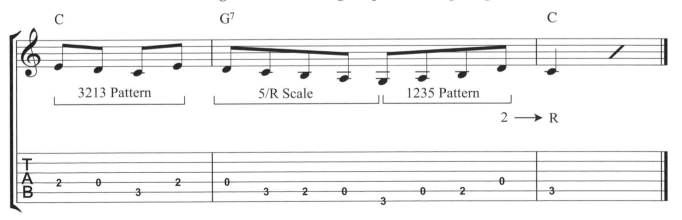

Other Useful Scale Fragments.

You will frequently run across scale fragments from the third of a Major chord <u>ascending</u> to the flatted seventh (3/b7 Scale), <u>or</u> vice versa (b7/3 Scale), both 3-beat, 5-note scale fragments:

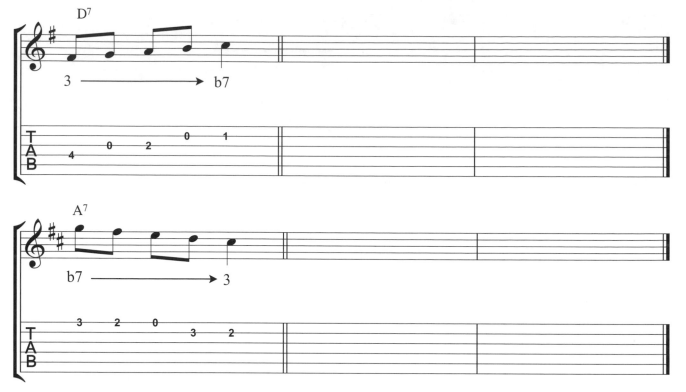

Should you need to fit this scale fragment into two beats, then you might consider using a 5321 digital pattern based on the flatted Seventh (this figure can also be used to substitute for a V7 chord outline):

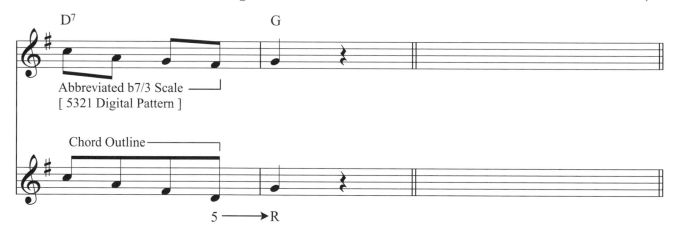

Here is an example, as played by Doc Watson, where he uses the b7/3 Scale fragment <u>twice</u> in the same phrase over a G7 chord:

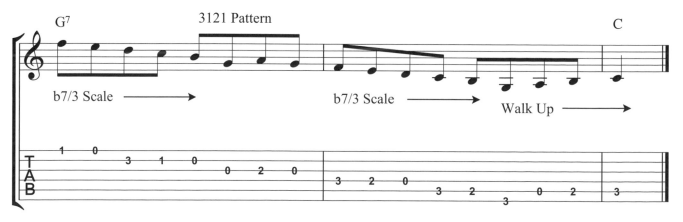

In this concluding example Doc Watson alters a descending mixolydian mode, based on the Third of the V7 chord (B natural) by introducing a leading tone to the flatted Seventh (E to F) that, in turn, disrupts the expected scale note sequence by creating an enclosure figure on beat 4 (note, however, that the concluding B natural still ends up correctly positioned on the last upbeat of the measure, i.e., the leading tone to the target note, C):

Nice work, Doc!

Scale Spins.

Scale spin fragments ascend or descend from a principal note, usually in intervals from a second to a fifth. A spin based an interval a second away is perhaps most easily described as an upper or lower neighbor tone, thus a 2-beat note sequence. Here are those examples:

In the following example a spin, based on the interval of a third over a V-I chord change, leads to a 5/R Scale:

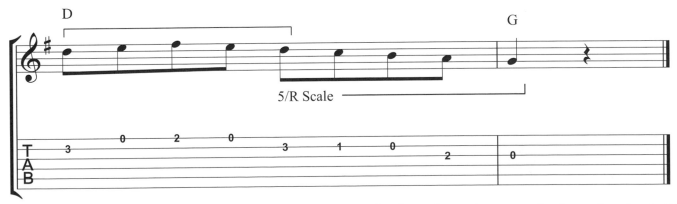

In a similar chord change the spin leads to a chord outline (in fact, the spin can substitute for the initial chord outline):

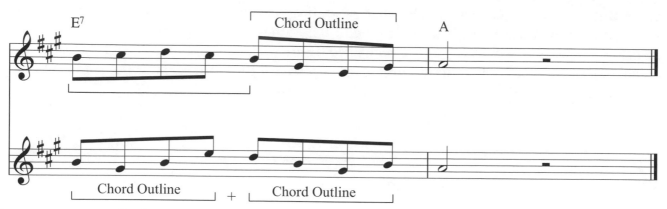

In this 2-measure example the spin figure is used twice in succession, leading to a R/5 Scale fragment:

In this example the spin is introduced on beat 3 of the initial measure:

As you have probably surmised, the spin note sequence is really based on passing tones. Here is the concept, based on the common fiddle cadence of R3R:

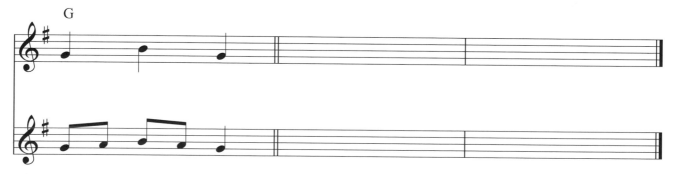

The use of a lower chord tone for the first passing tone is a common variation:

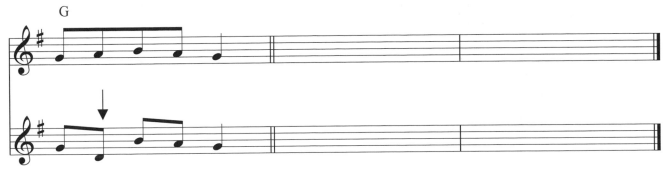

Let's now look at a couple of examples using the descending spin note sequence. The first example is based on the third of the G chord. In this case the last note of the spin coincides with a change of harmony, from G to D, by use of a common tone, i.e., B (which is sixth scale degree in D Major):

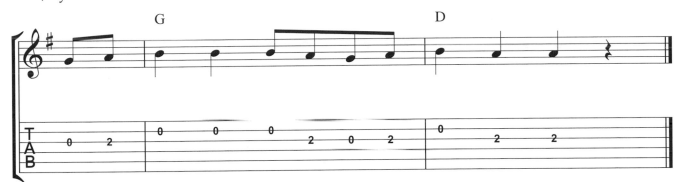

In the next example the descending spin figure leads to a 5/R Scale:

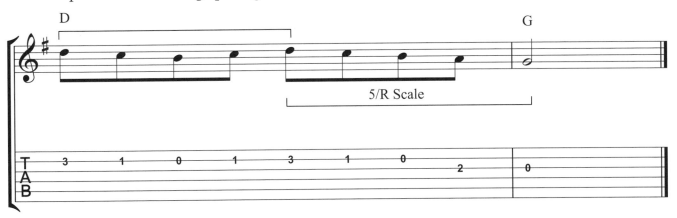

Most of the time ascending or descending spins seem to be able to be used interchangeably with regards to harmonic function.

Here is another example comparing the use of a spin for a chord outline (the common denominator being that the first note of the chord outline is identical with the initial note of the spin figure):

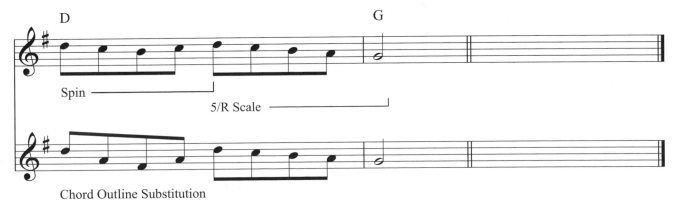

Now, let's look at several examples of how this descending spin figure is used in an ascending C Major scale; in all of these instances the spin figure is based on the fifth scale degree. In this example the scale spin simply interrupts the basic ascending scale line:

Here, the spin figure is repositioned to the downbeat of the second measure due to the use of two consecutive chord tone connector figures:

The first measure of the previous example can be painlessly varied by substituting ascending thirds for the two chord tone connector figures:

In this <u>descending</u> scale line the spin figure is introduced on beat 3 of the initial measure:

When discussing diatonic scales earlier I mentioned the alteration of the fifth and sixth scale degrees. Thus, if you would like to add a bit of chromaticism to scale lines, such as the four examples that I have just presented, then I suggest that you do it by altering the fifth note of the scale. Why the fifth scale degree? Simply put, because it is the second most important note in the scale (other than the Root itself).

The following signature bebop lick is loosely based on a 3-beat turn-like figure; for ease of sight reading purposes I have notated it as an Augmented Fourth (which is enharmonic with the flatted Fifth (i.e., F sharp is enharmonic with G flat):

Did you notice that I changed the ending slightly? I simply used the 1235 digital pattern based on the fifth note of the Major scale so that the target note was approached <u>from above</u> instead of from below, via the leading tone.

A spin, based on the interval of a fourth, takes up 4 beats, thus a full measure in Common time:

Likewise, the spin based on the interval of a fourth, takes up 5 beats. Here is an example:

Basically, spins are simply "filling up space" in a measure instead of just playing a sustained half note, etc.; spins can also be painlessly substituted for chord outlines.

The remainder of this book will basically revolve around the family of fragments that I call digital patterns, many of which share the same beginning and ending note (usually a 2-beat figure).

Digital Patterns.

The 1235 Digital Pattern.

As noted previously, this is a 2-beat pattern useful for outlining a chord, the only non-chord being the second note (identified here as a passing tone). Here is an example of this pattern outlining a G chord:

Often in a V-I cadence, because the Root of the V chord acts as a Common Tone with the fifth note of the tonic chord, you can target the Root of the tonic chord in two ways: by using the 1235 pattern, which leads to the octave of the chord <u>from</u> <u>above</u>, via the supertonic scale degree, or, by use of a descending 5/R Scale fragment:

The 1235 digital pattern can also be based on the fifth note of the tonic scale leading to the octave note (this leads to the same result as if that note was the fifth of the V chord, as just discussed).

If you wanted to target the fifth of the tonic chord, then you could also use the 1235 pattern beginning on the supertonic note of the scale, i.e., the second scale degree:

A word of warning here: the note sequence where the 1235 pattern is used <u>could</u> accidentally be analyzed as an A minor chord, thus the target note, D, would imply the arrival of the V chord, D Major. There is nothing inherently wrong about that, as the ii chord can lead to the tonic chord.

Now, let's look at a few ways that Doc Watson uses this pattern in his playing:

The 5321 Digital Pattern.

Where there is a 1235 pattern, there can also be a 5321 pattern. Because this pattern often begins on beat 3 remember that the target note, the Root, is going to be positioned on the upbeat of beat 4, <u>anticipating</u> the arrival of the Root. Here is such an example demonstrating that usage in the key of C:

Should you decide to target the Root on the downbeat using this figure, instead of anticipating it on the previous upbeat, you could, for instance, alter this digital pattern by adding a note, the third, on the last upbeat (instead of, perhaps, considering use of a 5/R Scale fragment to achieve the same result):

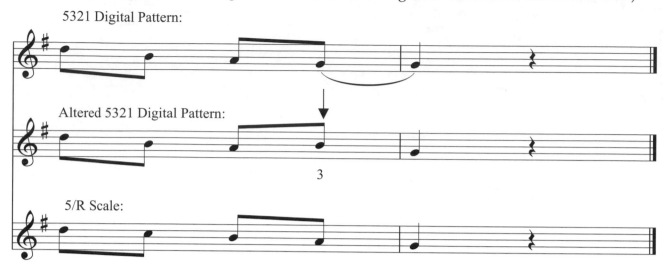

In this example the 5321 digital pattern is used to connect identical note sequences:

In the next example this pattern, used over the IV chord (C), segues painlessly into a 3217 1 cadential note sequence over the tonic G chord:

In the following example the target note of the 5321 digital pattern is the fifth of the G7 chord; thus, the pattern begins on the Ninth of the G9 chord. Here, this pattern leads to a 1231 digital pattern, then to an ascending Chord Tone Connector note sequence leading to the Root of the C tonic chord:

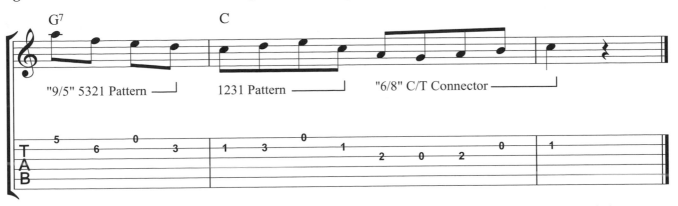

Had the note sequence begun on G, then a stock 5/R Scale fragment could have been used; however, the use of the Ninth results in a nice change of harmony for the ear.

Let's look at one way that Doc Watson uses this pattern in his playing (see the concluding measure):

The 1231 Digital Pattern.
This pattern is simply a scale fragment which goes up two notes, then returns to the original note. The initial note is usually based on the Root, third, or fifth of a chord.

We have seen this pattern used as a concluding tag in some of the previous examples. However, in this example it begins the phrase:

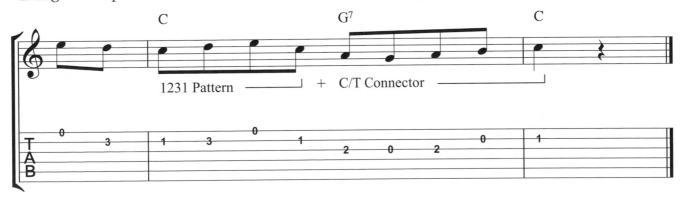

Here is a similar example where, this time, the 1231 pattern leads to a descending Chord Tone Connector which resolves to a stock fiddle cadence:

In this example, over a ii-V7 chord change, the 1231 pattern leads to a 5/R Scale fragment:

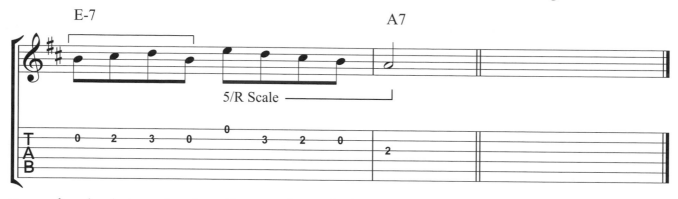

This pattern often leads to a chord outline, as shown below:

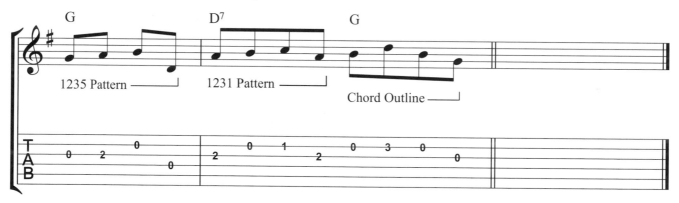

The 1231 pattern can also be altered rhythmically:

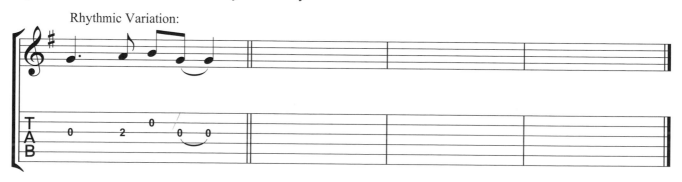

In the next example the 1231 pattern is used in succession over a IV-I chord progression:

This pattern can also be used over a V-I chord change; in fact, it can replace a 1235 digital pattern based on the Root of the V chord:

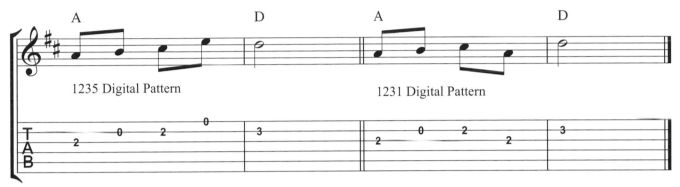

Let's look at a few commonly found variations. In the first example an ascending Chord Tone Connector leads to the 1231 pattern used as a tag, followed by a chord outline:

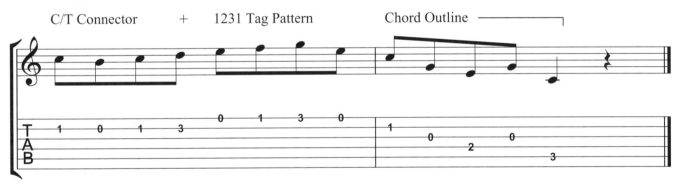

Next is an example where a R/5 Scale fragment leads to this pattern, once again used as a tag, followed by a stock fiddle cadential formula based on thirds:

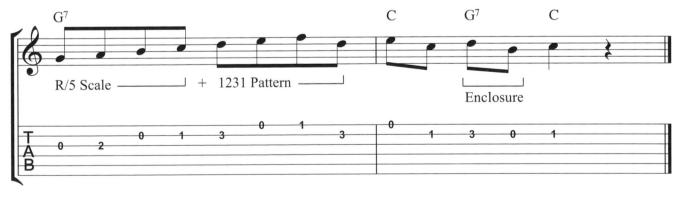

In this variation, an escape tone note sequence ends the phrase instead of a pair of thirds:

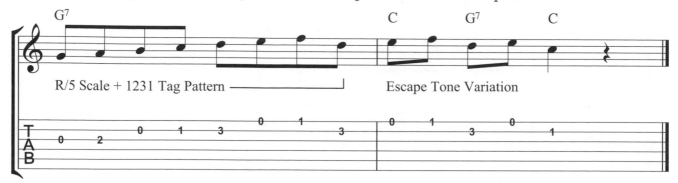

Similarly, in this example a 5/R Scale leads to the 1231 digital pattern tag ending:

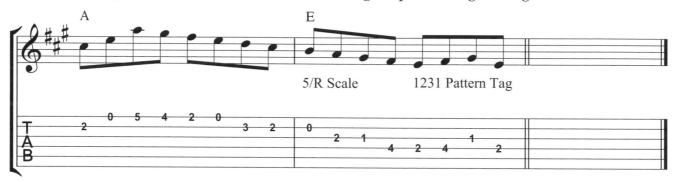

Now that you have the idea of how this digital pattern is used, let's look at some of the ways Doc Watson uses it in his playing:

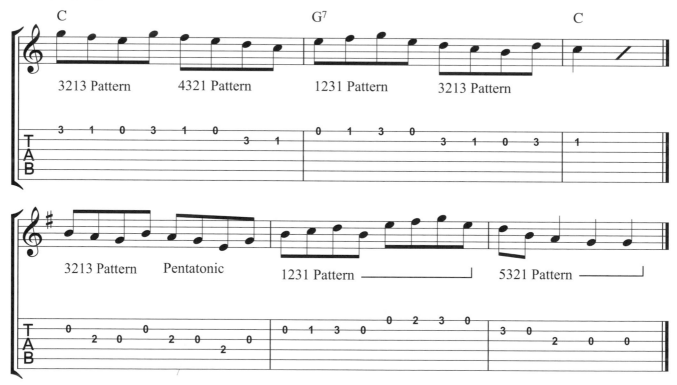

This pattern was used in an earlier Doc Watson example when I was outlining use of the 5321 digital pattern.

The 1321 Digital Pattern.

This note sequence is simply the reverse of the 1231 pattern. Here is an example which demonstrates how this pattern is commonly used:

Note how the last three <u>descending</u> notes of the 1321 pattern in this example lead naturally to the final two lower pitched notes in the measure; in fact, because the note after this pattern is A, a descending Chord Tone connector (C to A) could also have been used.

In the following example, the 1321 pattern is used over the IV chord leading to a 3217 1 note sequence over the V-I chord. A variation occurs, however, in that the arrival of the Root of the tonic chord is delayed by positioning the supertonic on the downbeat. Let's look at it:

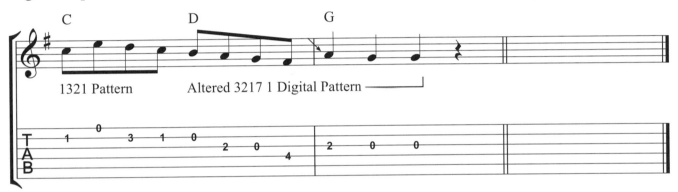

The 1321 pattern is also frequently used to "fill in" descending scale lines using longer rhythmic values. Here is such an example:

This pattern often acts as a tag, as has been shown previously. However, if you have skipped to this section of the book here is an example where this pattern follows an ascending Chord Tone Connector figure:

Here is a similar example over a V-I cadence:

The altered Turn Cadence could have also been used here just as well. Again, make note of the forward motion created by the descending scale of the last three notes of this pattern to smoothly target the Root of the G tonic chord; if the initial note of this pattern had been a D, then the note sequence would have been analyzed as a 5/R Scale fragment.

Speaking of turn figures, in the next example, where the intervallic distance between the initial note of the V7 chord and the Root of the tonic chord is a only a Major second, a turn figure based on the fifth of the E7 (V) chord is positioned on the downbeat leading to the 1321 digital pattern to painlessly bridge that short distance:

In the following example the 1321 pattern replaces a chord outline:

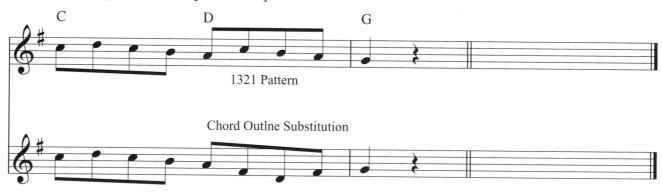

Finally, here is an example where the 1231 and 1321 digital patterns are used in tandem:

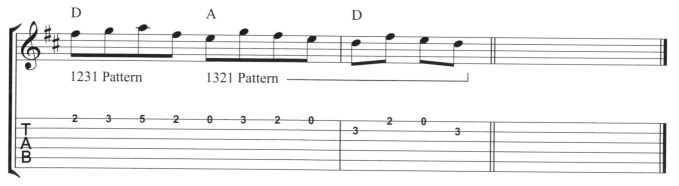

Let's now move on to the 3213 digital pattern.

The 3213 Digital Pattern.

This pattern descends the interval of a third and then returns to the principal note. Here is a basic example of this pattern positioned on the downbeat followed by a 5/R Scale note sequence, ending with a rhythmically varied 1321 digital pattern tag:

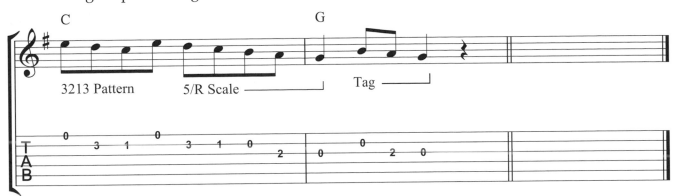

In the following example the R/5 Scale fragment leads to a 3213 digital pattern tag which then segues into an ascending Chord Tone Connector figure targeting the third of the F chord:

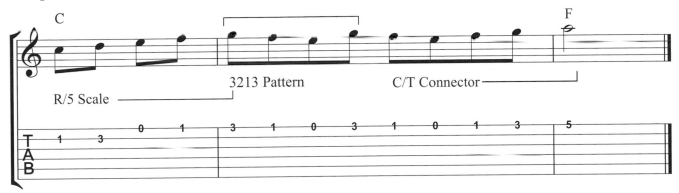

Next, this pattern acts as a tag following an ascending Chord Tone Connector (the 1321 digital pattern could just as easily have been used here):

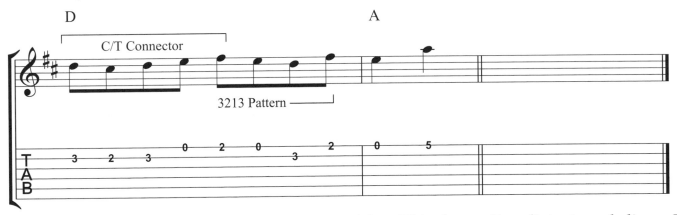

As shown earlier, this type of digital pattern is quite useful to fill in descending diatonic scale lines. Here are two examples:

Basic Line:

Basic Line:

3213 Patterns

5/R Scale

Doc Watson also uses this pattern frequently in his performance style. Here is one of the many ways in which he uses it:

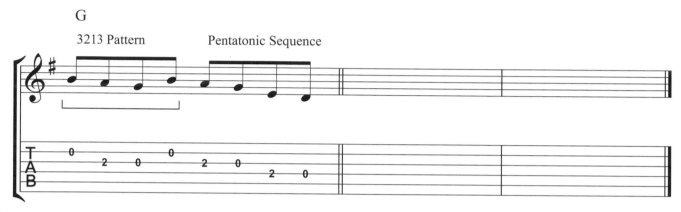

G

3213 Pattern   Pentatonic Sequence

The 1231 and 3213 digital patterns can be in tandem. Here are two such examples:

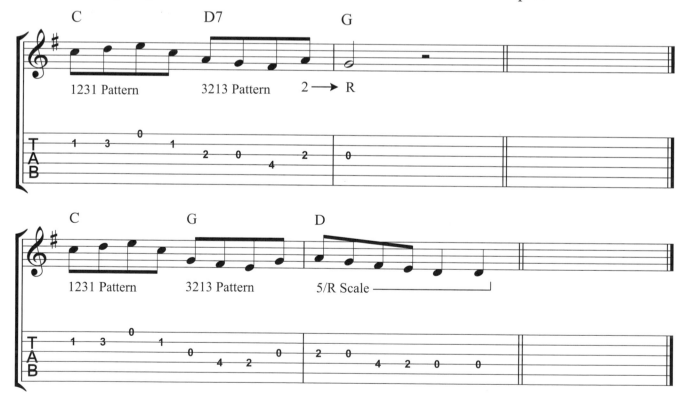

C   D7   G

1231 Pattern   3213 Pattern   2 ⟶ R

C   G   D

1231 Pattern   3213 Pattern   5/R Scale

The 3123 Digital Pattern.

The 3213 digital pattern can also be inverted into the 3123 digital pattern. Here are two such examples of that usage:

The 4321 Digital Pattern.

This pattern can be looked at as the descending lower tetra chord of the Major diatonic scale. The pattern is often positioned on beat 3 of a measure, targeting the Root of the chord that it is based on (however, the third or fifth can also be the target note). The pattern can be approached by a variety of note sequences, e.g., chord outlines, Chord Tone connectors, sequences of thirds, etc.; it can also be used to fill out descending scales, or to anticipate the arrival of the tonic note. Let's look at these various functions.

In the first example a D chord outline leads to the 4321 digital pattern which happens to create a 4-3 resolution leading to the third of the A chord (you might analyze this note sequence as a b7/3 scale fragment except that you would expect that usage over a V-I chord change, _not_ a I-V chord progression):

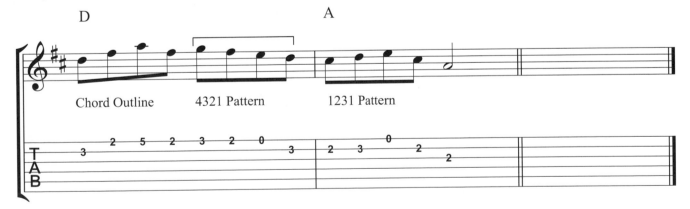

In the next example the third of the G chord, B, is the target note:

Here is an example which uses a descending Chord Tone Connector to lead to the 4321 pattern. The first note of that pattern is the Root of the C scale, not the fourth scale degree as might be expected:

In the following V7-I chord change the last note of the 4321 pattern <u>anticipates</u> <u>the</u> <u>arrival</u> of the Root of the tonic chord on the following downbeat, a common jazz performance practice (a similar practice was discussed earlier regarding the 5321 digital pattern):

Next are two examples of this pattern used over a V-I chord change. In the first example the 4321 pattern is used twice in succession; the second example is more conventional, i.e., a descending Chord Tone connector leading to the 4321 pattern.

Here is an example demonstrating the use of thirds as the approach vehicle to this pattern that targets the Root of the F minor chord:

F minor

Thirds   4321 Pattern

Let's now look at two examples where the first note in the phrase of a V7 chord is the flatted Seventh. In the first one, an abbreviated b7/3 scale fragment leads to the 4321 digital pattern while in the second one the pattern is used in succession, connected by a repeated note:

A⁷

Abbrv. b7/3 Scale

4321 Patterns

Here are two additional examples of 4321 digital pattern usage where "4" is the fourth scale degree positioned on the downbeat of each phrase:

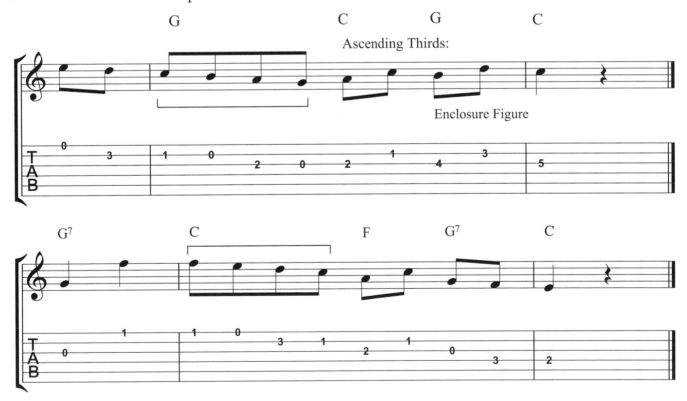

This digital pattern is yet another useful note sequence to "fill in" a descending scale, in this instance the melody voicing moves in half notes:

Here is an example where a number of the techniques that have been discussed are combined to form a phrase (take note that the first five notes resemble a 3217 1 note sequence; however, in that case the initial note would be analyzed as the Ninth of the A9 chord resolving on the flatted Seventh, G natural, on the downbeat):

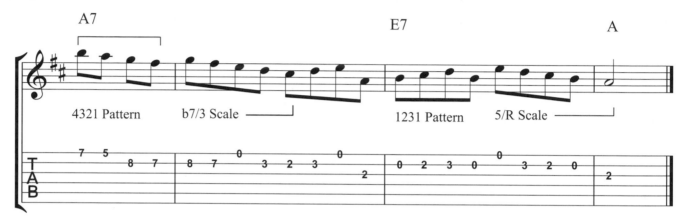

Let's close out this section by looking at one way that Doc Watson uses this pattern:

The Escape Tone Digital Pattern.
The way that I label this pattern does not exactly match that correct, classical theoretical definition; however, the basic result is the same, i.e., a descending diatonic scale line is interrupted. In the following example the melodic line of F# to E to D, is temporarily interrupted by a note positioned on the upbeat moving in contrary motion:

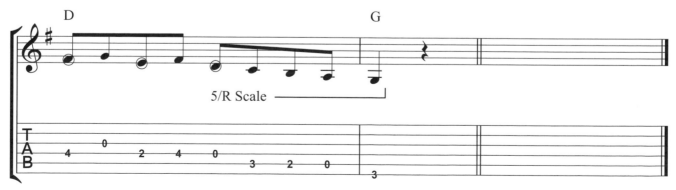

A descending chord tone connector could have been used for the Escape Tone note sequence. The reason it wasn't used is simply because the E, on beat 2, is part of the melodic line, thus we preserved the correct voice leading by using the escape tone pattern (if a Chord Tone connector had been used the E would have been replaced by an F#).

Let's look at a phrase which uses the escape tone pattern twice, thus a sequence:

If correct voice leading is not an issue then the use of intervals of a third, a commonly used fiddle cadential figure, can be painlessly substituted:

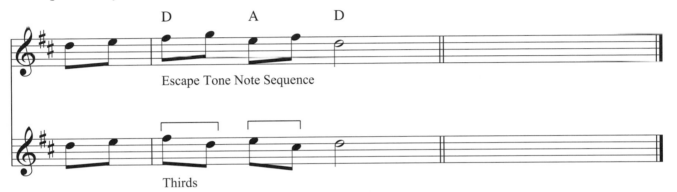

Escape Tone Note Sequence

Thirds

Likewise, you can also vary the third and fourth notes in the pattern by transposing them:

Here are three examples where the escape tone note sequence leads to different outcomes:

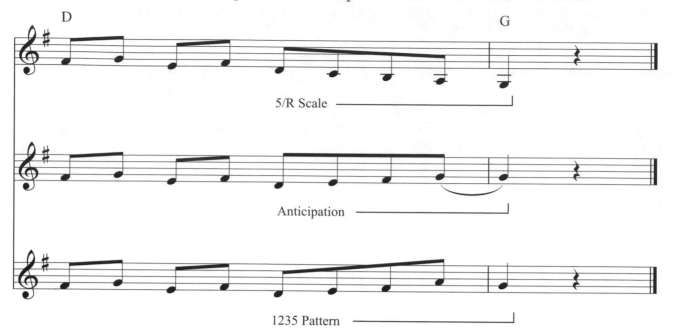

In the next example the phrase begins with a 3123 digital pattern, followed by a 4321 digital pattern which leads to the escape tone figure:

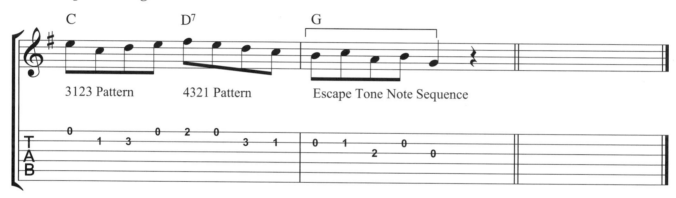

CULC Digital Pattern.

A note sequence which resembles an escape tone figure, in that the first and last notes are the same, consists of the following: Chord tone – Upper neighbor tone – Lower neighbor tone – Chord tone (I usually abbreviate this pattern as CULC).

The basic concept of the CULC can be applied to neighboring <u>chord tones</u>. Here are three examples:

The CLUC Digital Pattern.

If you transpose the CULC digital pattern you end up with a Chord tone – Lower neighbor tone – Upper neighbor tone – Chord tone note sequence, i.e., CLUC.

Here is a comparison where this pattern can be used to substitute for a chord outline by a simple rearrangement of the chord tones based on the CLUC pattern (note the ascending scale line on beats 1, 3, then the following downbeat):

Similarly, here is an oft used phrase where the lower chord tone is used to "fill out" the pattern:

Let's now move on and discuss the use of the interval of the third.

Intervals of a Third.

As demonstrated several times in this book, the use of thirds is commonly found at cadences in fiddle tunes. Here is a basic example with two additional variations based on altering the direction of the intervals:

The use of thirds is also found in scale lines as well. Here is an example of an ascending scale line where ascending Chord Tone Connectors <u>could</u> <u>have</u> <u>been</u> <u>used</u> to fill in the scale; instead, thirds are used (with two different concluding note sequences):

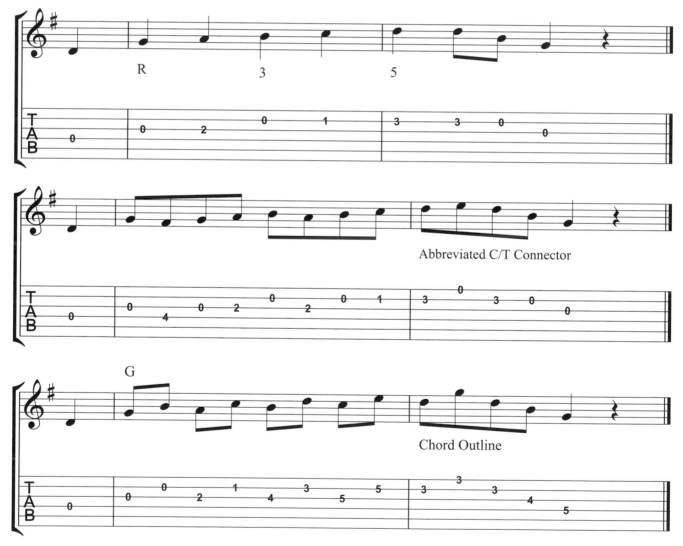

The lower note in the third pair can also be employed in ascending scale lines. Here is a comparison where first the lower note of the pair is used, then the higher note of the pair:

Thirds are frequently used to create harmonic interest in scale lines as well:

The Circle.

This is a note sequence where the notes "circle" the Root of a chord displacing its position from the expected downbeat to the upbeat. It is a 2-beat note sequence in which the initial note is often the half-step below, i.e., the leading tone, of the Root; the Root is then played, then the diatonic Upper neighbor tone, then a return to the Root. This note sequence is abbreviated as 7121. Here is an example:

In fiddle tunes, this note sequence is yet another way to "fill in" space in descending scales:

Repeated Notes.

In fiddle tunes repeated notes can often be found connecting the upbeat of beats 2 to 3. Compare this usage to a descending chord tone connector sequence with a scale tag:

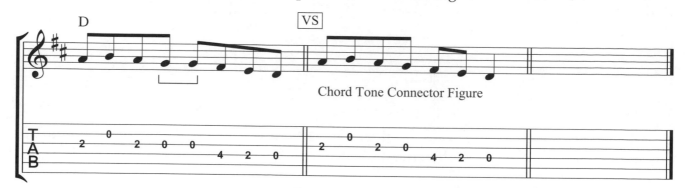

Chord Tone Connector Figure

Here is an example where the repeated note <u>crosses</u> the bar line:

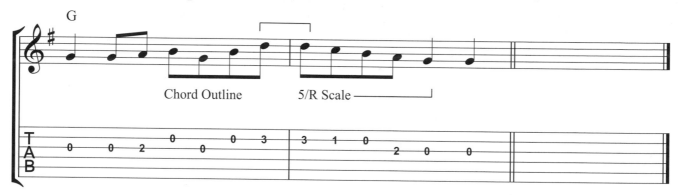

Chord Outline   5/R Scale

As you might expect, the second repeated note can also function as a common tone in a chord change. Here is such an example using chord outlines:

Here is a similar example (make particular note of the sequence used to outline the A7 chord, as well as the rhythmically altered 1321 digital pattern tag):

In this variation a similar V7 chord outline is used to target the Root of the tonic chord, C (note that a 5/R Scale note sequence could have been used instead of the V7 chord outline):

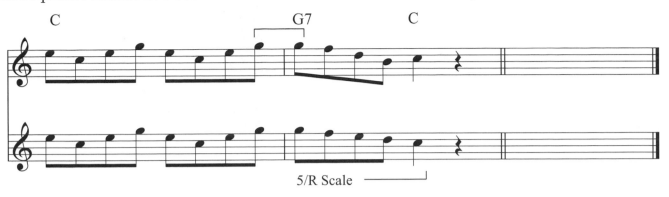

Painless Arranging: *Wreck of the Old 97.*

At the beginning of this book I showed how some of these painless arranging techniques were used in four fiddle tunes. If you played through them you should have noticed that there was a flow from note group to note group, phrase to phrase. This is your goal, as not all of these techniques will work seamlessly in context. By experimenting with them you will eventually choose the ones that sound best to your ear.

Let's now use what I have outlined by making a solo arrangement of a popular string band song, dating from around 1903 about a famous Danville, Virginia, train wreck, entitled *The Wreck of the Old 97.* This song seems to have been first recorded by Henry Whitter (later of Grayson & Whitter string band duo fame) in December 1923. This recording seems to have prompted Ernest V. Stoneman to become a professional musician as well, since Stoneman felt that he was a better vocalist and musician than Whittter was. However, Stoneman didn't get around to recording *Wreck* until January 27, 1927, for Okeh records. In any event, here are two choruses from that recording (the notational differences from chorus to chorus are based on different words and syllables):

Henry Whittier

The Wreck of the Old 97

This 8-measure song is based on the chord progression of a lot of folk songs: I IV I V followed by I IV V I. Vocal songs are often based on chord tones, thus making it easier to remember them. This arrangement presents many opportunities to painlessly vary the melodic line.

Let's look at the first chorus (section A1). The first thing to look out for are "holes" in the vocal line, i.e., beats where you can fill in or connect the melodic line because of longer note values at phrase endings. For instance, on beat 3 of the second measure you have a B followed by a D note; since these two notes are the first in a 1321 digital pattern you could consider using that note sequence to fill in beat 4 (as well as leading back to the following downbeat, A in the third measure):

At the half cadence at measure 4 the C#, the third of the A chord, eventually leads to the A on the upbeat of beat 4. Obviously, this intervallic distance is that of a third so you can easily fill that space in with a descending Chord Tone connector with a walk-up line to the Root of the D chord in the following measure:

The opening beats of measure 5 are D notes, so you could use a turn figure there:

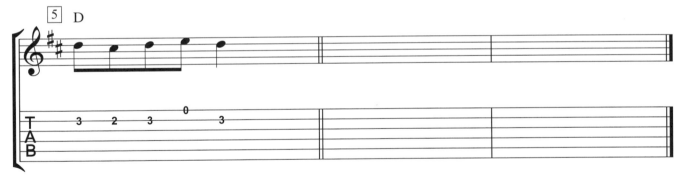

In measure 6 an ascending Chord Tone connector could be used to connect the G to B chord tones:

In measure 7 you could use a Doc Watson lick by using two Chord Tone connectors in succession to lead back to the Root of the tonic chord:

You might then consider using a pentatonic chord outline at measure 8:

Here is what you would have come up with:

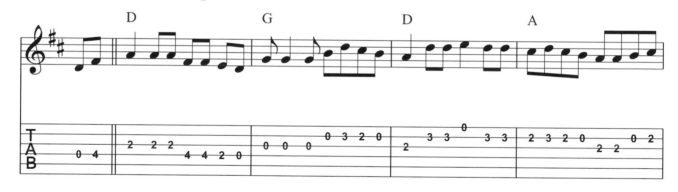

Now, I would like to present two additional choruses that I painlessly created:

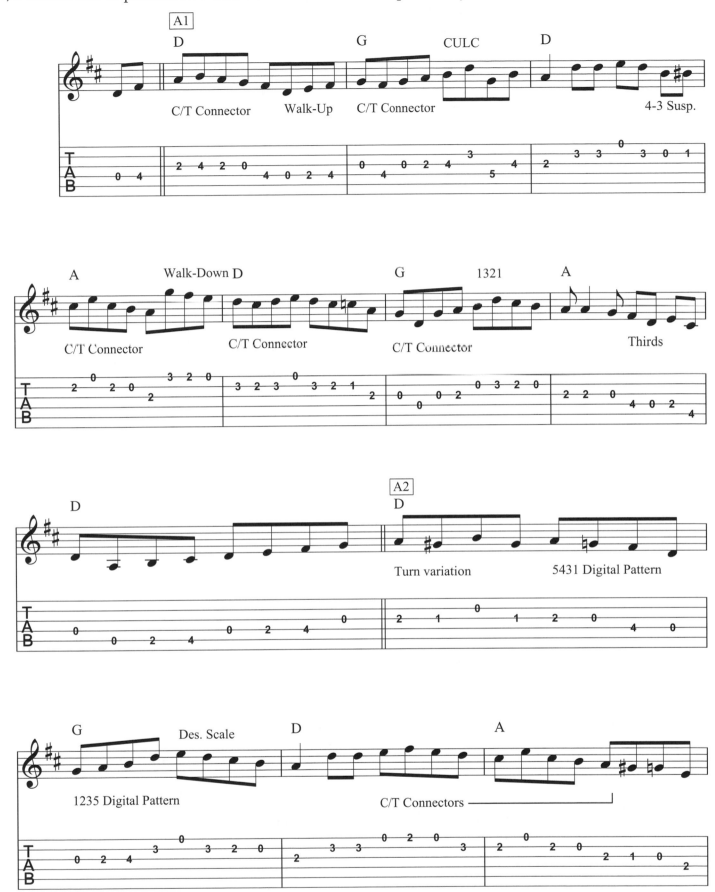

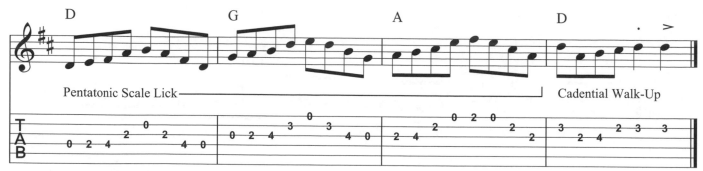

Let me explain to you what I did, and why.

Chorus 1. In the first measure I used a cadential figure that is frequently used in fiddle tunes in the key of G Major. This note sequence consists of a descending Chord Tone connector followed by a walk-up pattern.

I follow this up with an ascending Chord Tone connector to begin the second measure followed by a CULC digital pattern.

Measure 3 features a note sequence that I didn't cover in the body of the text which is a 4-3 suspension figure, i.e., the D, the fourth scale tone in the A Major scale, resolves downward one half-step to C#; this is very similar to the 7-3 tritone resolution in V7-I chord changes. However, in this instance I added a bebop jazz chromatic line that interrupted the direct 4-3 note resolution.

In measure 4 I use a varied descending Chord Tone connector by substituting a chord tone on the second note of the figure instead of the upper diatonic neighbor tone. I follow this with a walk-down line from the flatted Seventh of A to the Root of the D chord.

As the first notes in measure 5 are the same, D, a turn is a good figure to use here, followed by a chromatic line leading to the Root of the G chord on the downbeat of measure 6.

In measure 6 I, once again, use a varied descending Chord Tone connector followed by the 1321 digital pattern (note that in measure 2 I used the CULC note sequence).

In the following measure I used the common fiddle cadential note sequence of descending thirds that logically leads back to the Root of the tonic chord, D. At that point I used a walk-up pattern followed by a R/5 Scale fragment to lead to A natural on the following downbeat, which leads to the next chorus.

Chorus 2. To begin this chorus I began with an altered turn figure leading to a 5431 digital pattern; as it often happens, this pattern is aurally more pleasing than the more direct 5321 digital pattern. I do, however, use the 1235 digital pattern on the downbeat of measure 2 to outline the G chord followed by a 4321 digital pattern based on the sixth scale degree of G Major; this figure leads to A, the fifth of the D chord, on the downbeat of measure 3.

An E minor Seventh chord is implied on beat 3 of measure 3, thus I decided to use a descending Chord Tone connector that led to a 7-3 tritone resolution, D to C#, the third of A. The following measure uses that varied descending Chord Tone connector to a chromatic line leading to the Root of the D chord in measure 5.

For the next three measures I simply decided to use the same pentatonic note sequence over the D, G and A chords, then using a stock 5678 note sequence to end the chorus.

Conclusions.

I hope you can see that it was quite painless to create those variations. I simply looked at what the melodic line offered in terms of melodic intervals or patterns and filled in the gaps or slightly varied the melodic line to preserve its flavor.

You can painlessly create your own variations just as easily! That is why this book is called *Painless Arranging for Old Time Country Guitar.*

Joseph Weidlich
Washington, DC

The Beverly Hill Billies

More Great Guitar Books from Centerstream...

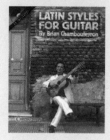